TEXTURE: A Design Element

Detail of woven collage showing use of seaweed and driftwood incorporated into the fibers of jute, hemp and yarns; by Olga Magnone. Photograph by David Donoho and courtesy of Doris Standerfer, Professor of Art, San Jose State College, California.

TEXTURE: A Design Element

George F. Horn
Coordinator of Art
Baltimore City Public Schools
Maryland

Davis Publications, Inc.
Worcester, Massachusetts

Copyright 1974
Davis Publications, Inc.
Worcester, Massachusetts, U.S.A.

Printed in the United States of America
Library of Congress Catalog Card Number: 74-82683
ISBN: 0-87192-066-2

Printing: Davis Press, Inc.
Type: Theme Medium
Graphic Design by: The Author
Consulting Editors: Gerald F. Brommer, Sarita R. Rainey

10 9 8 7 6 5 4 3 2

CONTENTS

TEXTURE —*Our world*   7
TEXTURE —*Surface quality, real and implied*   24
TEXTURE —*Another dimension*   34
TEXTURE *and light, structure, pattern*   36
TEXTURE *and the artist*   45
TEXTURE *and man, the creator*   57

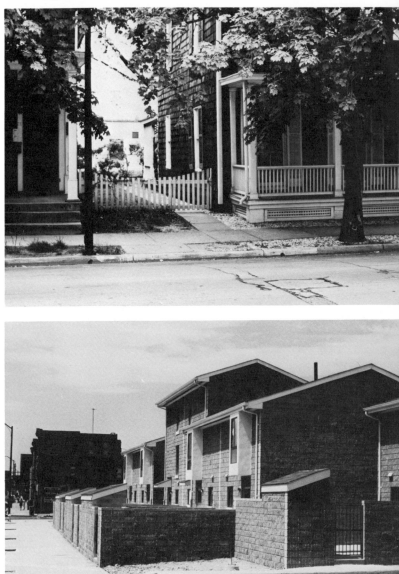

6

TEXTURE...
our world

Your home, your backyard, the street in front
of your house, the community that you live in —
Your church — and school
and the sky above —
and all other corners of the world
in which you breathe and move and enjoy —
or dislike —
and study, play and work —
or just "hang around" —
all become a reality through those visual elements
that give form to things and objects —
people and animals and other creatures
and non-creatures —
walls, floors, windows and furniture
rugs, draperies and a color TV
a fence, a sidewalk, a chimney, a gnarled tree —
and an old gray cat —
a super jet etching its white vapor trail in
a deep blue sky.

As you walk or ride from home to school
or to a friend's house or the playground —
or even if you are running an errand to
the local supermarket —
how many different shapes and colors do you see?

How many lines?
And what different feelings do you sense as your
path takes you over grass or cement?
A gravel walkway or eight inches of new-fallen snow?
What variety of sensations do you encounter
as you ride a bike
or skate on a coarse, macadam street
or a stretch of concrete paving that is patterned
with time-wrought cracks and crevices?

When you pause to rest —
and place your hand against the craggy trunk
of an ancient tree —
or stoop to pet a friendly dog —
or inadvertently slide your hand across the
plate glass window of the local dress shop
as you examine the splendid models on display —
are you aware of the dissimilarities
of the surfaces that you touch?

At seven thousand feet, an overwhelming sense of space as the brilliant sun is reflected on clouds, bay and serpentine rivers.

A non-objective pattern of soft snow on the ice of a partly frozen lake.

Each of the parts of our total environment
has an identity
that is revealed to us by its blueness
or redness
or chartreuseness!
By its largeness, smallness or squareness.
By spaciousness and closeness
and the diversity of line that describes, encircles,
directs —
By roughness, softness, smoothness —

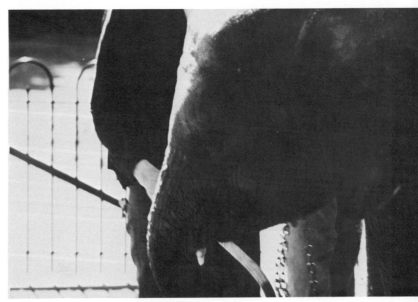

A young elephant poses his wrinkled face.

Gone to seed, these dandelions present a fluffy series of soft balls.

Coarse building blocks, joined by mortar, give a Mondrian-like design.

Seagull, wet sand and a reflection.

Our ability to see and hear smell, taste and feel
enables us to experience the wonder and
delight of our world —
and to recognize its ugliness and deterioration, too!

LOOK closely
at your world!
And experience the thrill of countless patterns —
of line, shape, space, color, value
and texture —
as you come into contact with them day by day.

16

"Pretty Fish," ceramic by Peggy Jones, Lutheran High School, Los Angeles, California.

An assortment of tools (sticks, knives) were used to create an interesting pattern of texture on the surface.

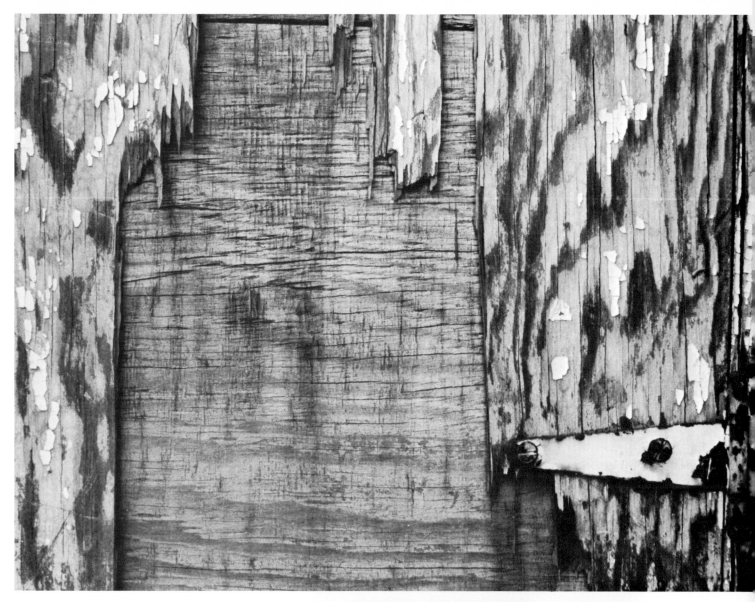

The visual elements —
line, shape, space, color, value
and texture —
exist in combinations.

For example,
a red ball is not just the *color* red
but it also has a round *shape* and is
actually a spherical form
with a smooth (texture) surface.
You will become more aware of this interaction of the
visual elements as you relate more intently to anything
and everything around you and
as you go through this book
which will focus on
the many TEXTURES of our world.

Detail, George Eastman Memorial Building, Rochester Institute of Technology; John Dinkeloo and Associates of Hamden, Connecticut, Architects.

Basically, stark, flat surfaces these walls have a subtle texture of brick and mortar.

Turtle, attracted by food, stretches his craggy head out from his hard, almost impenetrable shell.

A famous old clock with textured support contrasts with the background of new architecture.

Utility pole and wires, silhouetted against the sky, create a striking linear pattern.

A tremendous quarry carved into the surface of the earth reveals a variety of textures.

Given emphasis by new fallen snow, this automobile junk yard is a design in line and texture.

Man's thoughtlessness has resulted in a textured pollution of this harbor's water.

23

TEXTURE...
surface quality,
real and implied

Cutting through the surface to widen a road, this bulldozer uncovers a variety of real textures: stone, brick, concrete and dirt.

The smoothness of playground equipment invites children to the top.

The special texture of the green grass of the golf course provides the golfer with encouragement as he attempts a putt.

TEXTURE is a part of us at all times —
Even when we sleep and rest our weary bodies
on *smooth* sheets
and a *soft* bed
with tired head comfortably placed
on a *fluffy* pillow!

When we dress, if that blouse, shirt or collar
has too much starch or some *jagged* areas,
we experience a *scratchiness* that is uncomfortable.

Have you walked barefooted through the house
and noticed the different sensations as your feet
come in contact with the *hard* wood floor, tiles
or *soft,* pleasant carpeting?
And how many times have you cheered the home
ball team to victory from the vantage
point of *rough, grainy* wood bleachers?
How does it feel
when you put your hands into a pair of
fur-lined gloves on a cold, wintry day?
Pull a coarsely woven, woolen sweater
over your head?
Wash your hands with a *slippery* bar of soap?
Chase a beach ball over a sandy beach
on a hot summer day?
Rub your fingers over a piece of coarse sandpaper?

*Climbing equipment on the playground is
constructed of different kinds of textures.*

26

A gravel filled area contrasts with the smoothness of the sidewalk.

A smooth surface is important to devotees of this popular pastime.

Silken feathers against a background of grass and cut-stone wall.

A recent rainfall left this puddle of water, its smooth surface reflecting a partial image of a building and a flag.

The mirror-like texture of plate glass reflects cars, trees and a monument.

These are just a few examples of encounters we may have with TEXTURE in our daily lives.
As we become more aware of the characteristics of our natural and man-made environment, we will understand:

—That TEXTURE is a surface quality, related closely to our sense of touch.
—That various things and objects around us feel differently as we come in physical contact with them.
—That the quality of TEXTURE may range from hard to soft, smooth to rough, wet and slippery to dry and, sometimes, sticky!
—That TEXTURE is another dimension that helps to identify or describe something; a rock as *smooth* or jagged; a piece of cloth, soft or harsh; a wet street, slippery.
—That some TEXTURES are soothing, pleasant and draw us to them; others, abrasive, unpleasant and repelling.
—That pronounced TEXTURES attract attention; subtle and smooth TEXTURES are quieter and more reserved.
—That words such as smooth, slick, glazed, shiny, silky, velvety, soft and fluffy stimulate a range of tactile (touch) sensations that contrast with words like hard, jagged, abrasive, granular, rugged, craggy, bristly. All of these words are descriptive of the world of TEXTURE. Perhaps you can think of others.

A fluffy, soft ball of seeds suspended at the end of a long stem.

Below: The texture of mortar contrasts with brick in the wall of this house.

A weathered piece of metal has a corroded texture of its own.

Up to now we have been discussing TEXTURE as a tactile or touch sensation. But it really is more than that!
If you pause and re-read some of the words (above) describing TEXTURE,
you will note that you can sense TEXTURE without actually touching something or without moving your hand
over a textured surface. The same is true if you turn and look at the glass windows in your art room or tile mosaic displayed on the bulletin board. You can "feel" with your eyes the smoothness of the glass windows and the irregularity of the tiles set in the mosaic design.

This is a result of previous experiences with TEXTURE combined with your ability to see and interpret.
The world of TEXTURE, then,
becomes a reality to us, not only through our sense of touch,
but also through our sense of sight and our increasing understanding of the structure of things around us.

An additional aspect of our search for and discovery of various TEXTURES is that many times we see and become aware of TEXTURES that are not actually there!

Refer to the pages of this book which contain photographs of a diversity of TEXTURES.
Select what appears to be the roughest one and rub your fingers over it.
You "know" that it is a rough TEXTURE but you cannot feel it.
All that you can feel is the surface of the paper on which the photograph is printed.
We are now talking about *implied* TEXTURE.
The artist and illustrator often use the technique of manipulating lights and darks, lines and colors to represent TEXTURES that produce a quality of realism in a painting or illustration.
And designers, stylists and architects frequently use materials that have relatively smooth surfaces but appear to be TEXTURED.
Look around you and see how many examples of implied TEXTURE you can find.

30

Ceramic turtle by a student, Lutheran High School, Los Angeles, California.

The linear design on the shell and the knobby texture of the legs give this turtle a life-like appearance.

The strength and agelessness of this ancient oak are emphasized by the sharp, craggy texture of its bark.

Number I. 1948. Jackson Pollock, oil on canvas, 68" x 104". The Museum of Modern Art, New York.

One of the visual qualities of this painting is the textural effect achieved by the artist.

Whale II. Alexander Calder. (1937; this is the second version, 1964); stabile; painted sheet steel, 68 x 69½ x 45 3/8. Gift of the artist (by exchange). The Museum of Modern Art, New York.

33

The smooth, painted surface of this stabile emphasizes the stark simplicity of its shapes.

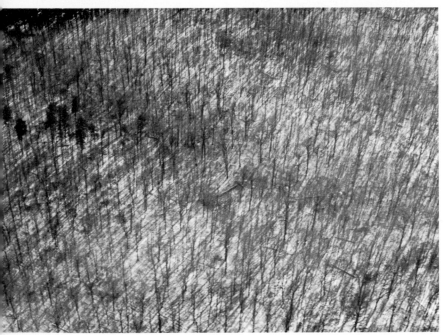

TEXTURE...
another dimension

The images of our environment
take on new characteristics in relation to
our visual point of view.
This may vary
with the seasons of the year, weather conditions,
atmosphere and the position of the sun in the sky —
to create unusual TEXTURED patterns
that may be soft or harsh,
reflective and absorbing, dramatic.
The photographs on these pages were taken
from between one thousand and fifteen hundred feet
above the earth's surface.
They illustrate a variety of
interesting TEXTURES
from the soft, warm mantle of summer's trees
to the bristling linear design
of a barren, wintry woodland —
and the angular corrugations
of plowed fields, given emphasis by a new-fallen snow.

Man, in his quest
for comfort, mobility, recreation
and the better life —
has left his mark on the earth's surface,
which, when viewed from above,
presents a whole new realm
of TEXTURE and pattern.
This is well-illustrated by the four
photographs on the opposite page
shot from an airplane at one thousand feet, or less,
above ground level.
How many different TEXTURES do you see?
Note in particular
the crowded coastal resort town
with buildings constructed to the edge of the sea.
From this point of view
houses are no longer houses
but have become the warp and weft
of a roughly woven fabric,
dominated by the linear diagram
of a network of roads.
How does the TEXTURE of the surrounding ocean
differ from that of the city
fashioned by man?

Quarries, though necessary to support man's life style, leave huge textured scars on the earth's surface.

On cold, wintry days ice forms interesting textured patterns on the water's surface of a hydro-electric dam.

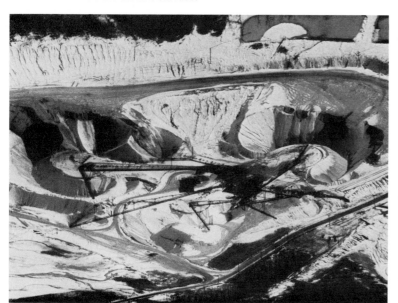

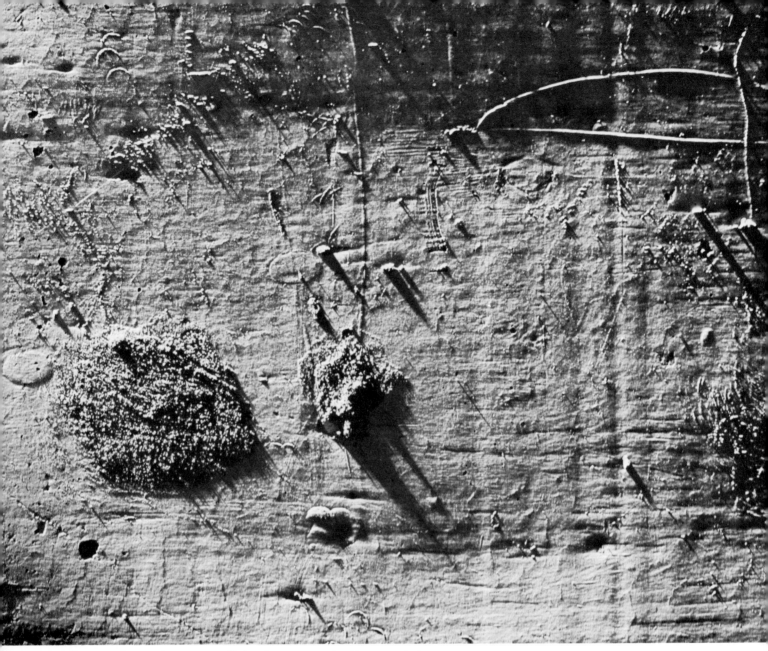

Section of poured concrete wall showing a textured pattern, created by the wood used in making the form.

TEXTURE
and light,
structure,
pattern

The many patterns of TEXTURE
are a result of the structure of the surface
of things and the light that is reflected.
No matter what degree of TEXTURE
a surface may have,
in the absence of light there is nothing
for the eye to detect.
Therefore TEXTURES will change
in relation to the strength of the light source
and the angle at which the light
contacts the TEXTURED surface.
A single TEXTURED surface,
rough or smooth,
can have many variations in its appearance
through changes
in the strength, concentration or diffusion
and position of the light source.

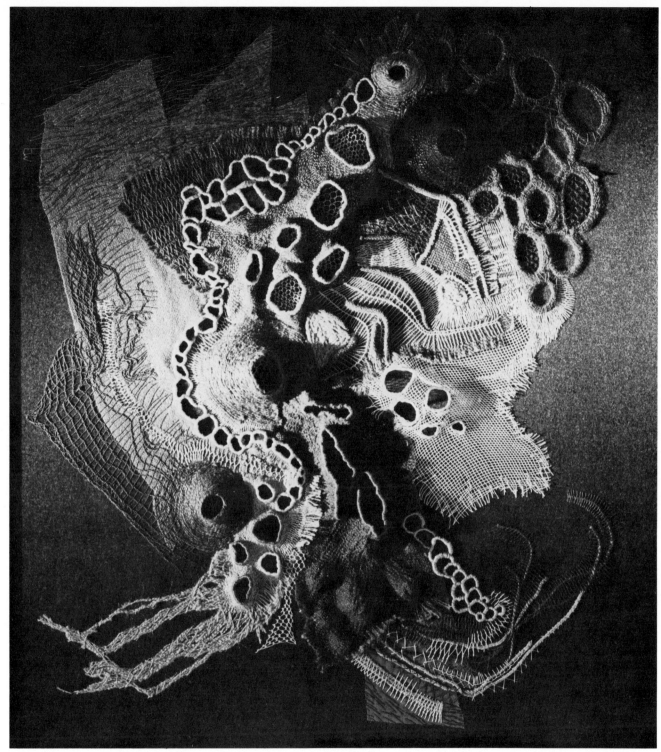

Gray Morning by Evelyn Svec Ward. Stitching, cutwork, appliqué; 32" h. x 3" w. The Museum of Contemporary Crafts.

A strong light from above emphasizes the varying textures of cloth and stitches.

A roughly TEXTURED surface
with a strong sidelight
will present a variety of sharply contrasting
shadows and highlights.
Glaring, even blinding flashes of light
will bounce off highly polished, shiny surfaces.
Smooth, satiny surfaces are characterized
by their soft, subtle reflection of light.

Our natural environment is comprised of
an endless pattern of TEXTURES.
Look around you.
Examine your world and note
the many different patterns of TEXTURE
that exist.
Look closer.
Study the structure of natural objects —
and the way in which light combines with
the surfaces of these forms
to create contrasting sensations of TEXTURE.

The texture of an orchard as seen from a height of fifteen hundred feet.

Prickly texture of a cactus.

Prints left by a seagull add texture to the smooth sand on the beach.

The texture of clam shells against the grain of wooden steps.

The texture of urban sprawl.

The artist is knowledgeable of
the many possibilities for achieving
different TEXTURAL qualities with materials —
to enhance his visual statement.
The finished product of the artist —
depending on the materials used,
the structure of the form
and the light that surrounds it —
will have a TEXTURAL pattern
that may range from extremely delicate
to decidedly dramatic features.

Section from panel titled La Liberté by Jordi Bonet, Canada.

Different textures have been developed by building up as well as cutting or stamping into the concrete surface.

Shadow of the Miracle by Zoltan Kemeny, Swiss, born in Hungary, 1907. Copper mounted on wood; 33 5/8 x 21 7/8. Gift of G. David Thompson. The Museum of Modern Art, New York.

Strong shadows created by the copper shapes present a strong pattern of texture.

Handcrafted ceramic objects, California Design Exhibit, Pasadena Museum of Art, California, showing a variety of textured patterns.

Collection, 1964, by Arman (Armand Fernandez), French, born 1928. Toy automobiles and boxes, 16 7/8 x 27 3/4 x 2 7/8. Promised gift and extended loan from Mr. and Mrs. William H. Copley. The Museum of Modern Art, New York.

Many small, individual pieces have been organized so that together they reflect a unique surface of texture.

Triptych in the Grand Theatre, Quebec City, Canada, Jordi Bonet, shows a variety of textures achieved by adding to and carving into the clay surface.

TEXTURE
and
the artist

Paints, inks, charcoal, pencil, chalk,
papers, boards, canvas —
stone, metal, wood, plastics, glass,
wet clay, glazes —
fibrous materials and dyes.
These are the materials of the artist —
shaped, combined and organized by him
to give visual life to an idea —
to record a moment in time.
Each of these materials is characterized
by its inherent qualities
of color, plasticity or non-plasticity,
and TEXTURE —
and varying indigenous limitations,
counterbalanced by potentialities
which are explored by the creative mind
of the artist —
who often works with such daring and boldness
as to appear somewhat contemptuous
of the materials that he is using.
Yet the artist is mindful
of how he may utilize materials
and the qualities they contain
to achieve completeness in his visual expression.

Wire sculpture by a student, Lutheran High School, Los Angeles, California. Liquid metal was added to the wire structure and allowed to harden. This was then buffed with steel wool giving a smooth quality to the high points in contrast with the roughness of the crevices.

45

Sojourner Truth and Booker T. Washington, pencil drawing by Charles White, American artist born in 1918. The Newark Museum, New Jersey.

The skillful use of the pencil by the artist has resulted in the illusion of many different textures in this composition.

TEXTURE, a surface quality,
appears in the work of the artist
in one of two basic ways:

a. *Implied TEXTURE*

TEXTURAL illusions, a sense of texture
or texture represented —
is more frequently associated
with drawings, paintings and prints —
in which the artist seeks to present
a spirit of realism or a feeling for TEXTURE
by manipulating the materials with which he works —
on a relatively flat surface.
Through the skillful and knowledgeable use
of paints, inks and drawing tools
the artist can create
the illusion of rough or smooth TEXTURES
on his canvas, or on paper —
He can represent the grain of wood,
the lines in a tired face —
the softness and sheen of silky cloth —
the reflective quality of glass.
The knots and roughness of wood
generally play an important role
in the ultimate print from a woodcut.
Strong TEXTURAL illusions
may also be a dominant feature in the works
of the non-objective painter,
where no attempt is made
to represent figures or objects
in a lifelike manner —
but rather to project a sensation
of roughness or smoothness
or some other TEXTURAL transformation
of a flat surface,
to give completeness
to an abstract idea.

Drawing, Italian, 20th Century. Marino Marini, Man and Horse, 1947. Watercolor and black ink. Nelson and Juanita Greif Collection, The Museum of Modern Art, New York.

An exciting textural effect has been achieved by the close arrangement and direction of fine lines combined with the bold, dry-brush strokes that seem to give structure to the drawing.

Woodcut by student, Lutheran High School, Los Angeles, California, showing the textural qualities of wood in the print.

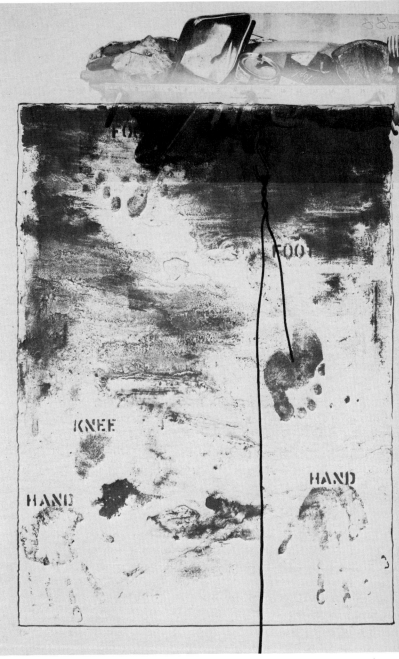

Pinion (Self portrait: foot, knee, hand) Jasper Johns, 1965-66. Lithograph, printed in color, 38 9/16" x 24½". Gift of the Celeste and Arwand Bartos Foundation. The Museum of Modern Art, New York.

Actual impressions of foot, knee and hand leave their unique textures on this interesting work of art. This, again, is an illusion of texture.

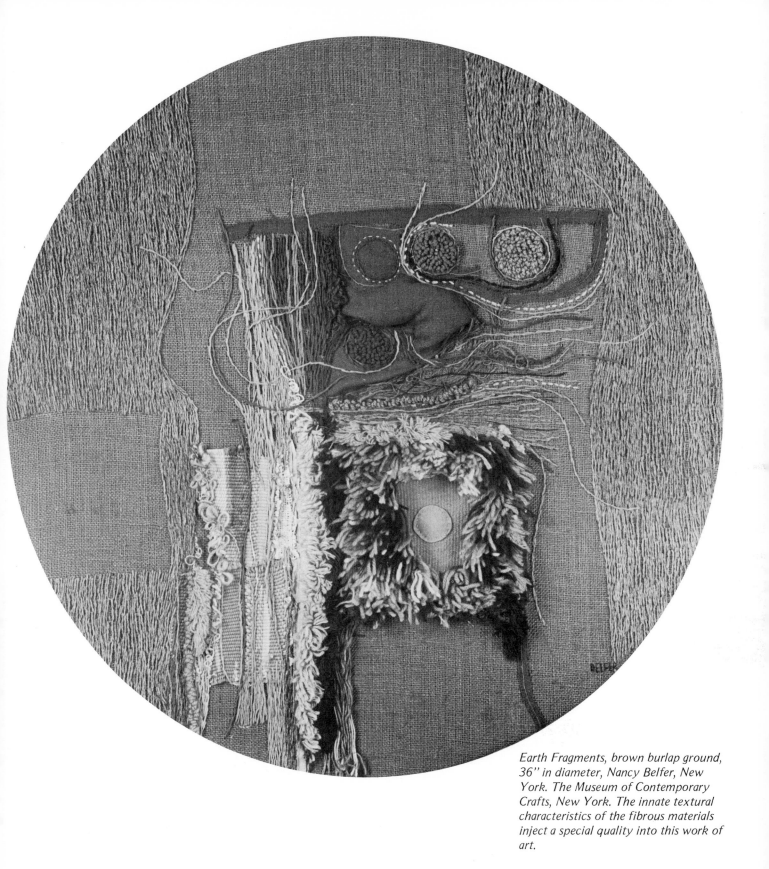

Earth Fragments, brown burlap ground, 36" in diameter, Nancy Belfer, New York. The Museum of Contemporary Crafts, New York. The innate textural characteristics of the fibrous materials inject a special quality into this work of art.

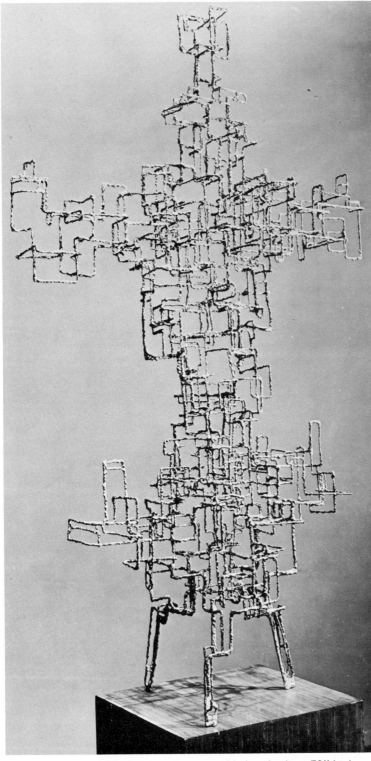

Kwannon. 1952, Ibram Lassaw. Bronze welded with silver, 72" high. The Museum of Modern Art, New York.

The application of silver with a welding torch gives an attractive rough quality to this linear sculpture.

b. *Actual or real texture*

The native TEXTURAL characteristics
of some materials used by the artist,
inject a special quality into
the product that he creates.
And as he interacts with materials
he controls and shapes them —
and they, in turn, influence him.
These materials lend themselves
to a variety of TEXTURAL finishes. .
A slab of stone may be carved and chiseled
and polished to the smoothness of glass —
or it may be roughened
to produce an entirely different effect.
Metal may be cut, bent, joined, hammered
and brazed to achieve varying
TEXTURAL features —
But metal, too, may be polished —
even to a mirror-like finish.
Some metals used in environmental sculpture
are allowed to weather, assuming TEXTURAL
changes over the years.
The plasticity of clay
provides the artist or craftsman
a wide choice of TEXTURAL finishes —
from smooth to rough as he leaves his mark
on the surface of the finished product.
Wood, glass, plastic, fibrous materials —
and the paint of the painter —
all have potential for a range of actual TEXTURES
which affect the appearance
of the work of the artist.

Plaster carving, student, Northern High School, Baltimore City, Maryland. Plaster with no additives (sand, sawdust, Vermiculite) presents a subtle textural quality in the surface of this carving.

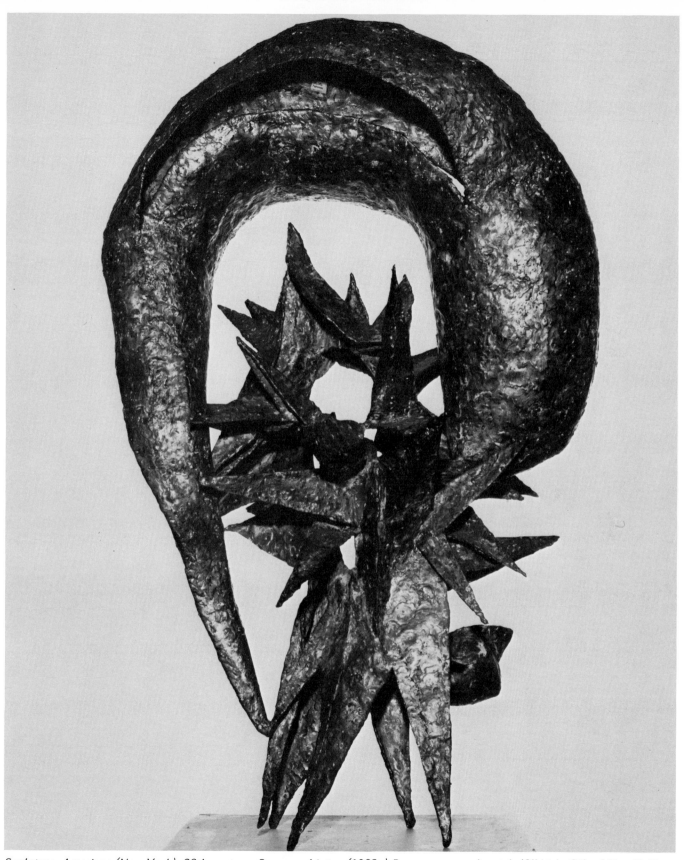

Sculpture, American (New York), 20th century. Seymour Lipton (1903-) Bronze on monel metal; 43" high. Gift of Mrs. F. W. Hilles in memory of her parents, Dr. and Mrs. William Inglis Morse and of Dr. and Mrs. A. R. L. Dohme. The Baltimore Museum of Art, Maryland.

The roughened surface of this sculpture reflects unusual patterns of light.

Temple mask, India. Photograph by Ferdinand Boesch. The Museum of Contemporary Crafts, New York.

A smooth, shiny surface reflects strong and sometimes harsh highlights.

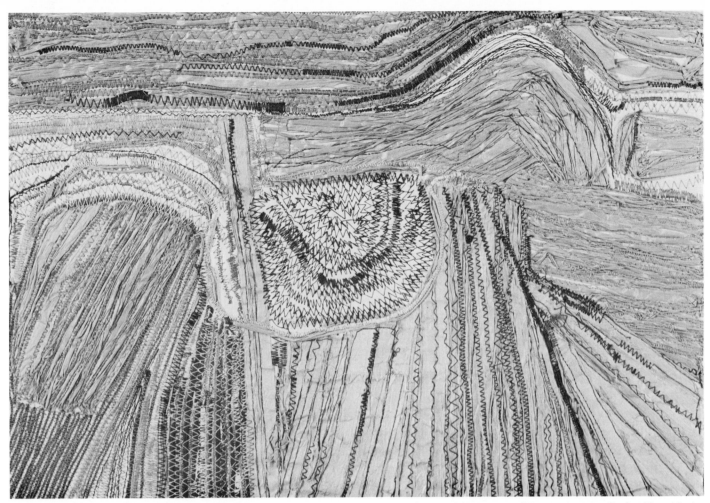

Landscape, natural raffia, machine stitchery, 20" x 20". Adrienne Kraut, Michigan. The Museum of Contemporary Crafts, New York. The natural qualities of materials and the varied assortment of stitches combine to create a moving textural design.

Wire sculpture, student, Lutheran High School, Los Angeles. A limited use of liquid metal emphasizes the strength of the coiled wire understructure and the rough texture of the animal.

Ceramic sculpture, student, Lutheran High School, Los Angeles, California. A pointed stick was used to create a texture that contributes to a spirit of realism in this sculptured animal.

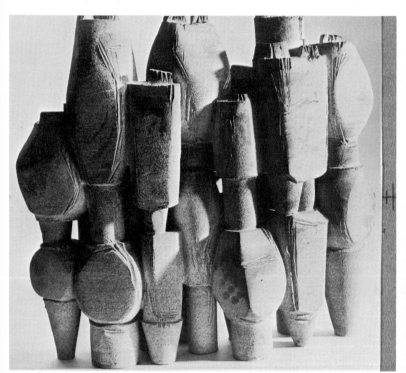

Stoneware cluster, courtesy of Architectural Pottery, Los Angeles, California.

While still in a semi-hard condition and before being joined, these clay sections were textured and shaped with a wooden paddle.

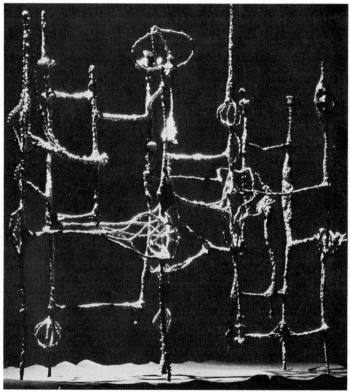

The Planets, 1954. Sculpture, American, 20th Century. Ibram Lassaw (1913 —). Medium: various bronzes. Height c. 36 3/8'', length c. 37''. Museum purchase. Charles and Elsa Hutzler Memorial Collection. The Baltimore Museum of Art, Baltimore, Maryland.

Strong top lighting of this linear sculpture gives emphasis to the textures created with a welding torch.

*Materials used by
the artist lend
themselves to
a variety of
TEXTURAL finishes*

*Two Lines — Temporal 1. 1964. Stainless steel 35' 2 3/8" high. George Rickey. Collection Mrs. Simon
Guggenheim Fund. The Museum of Modern Art, New York.*

The buffed aluminum surface is highly reflective of the strong sunlight.

Photograph courtesy of AIA Information Service, Washington, D.C.
Glass, metal, stone and concrete add varying textures to the work of the architect.

TEXTURE
and man
the creator

Preservation, conservation, renewal —
Landscaping, planting and green areas —
Environmental sculpture, fountains,
street furniture, lighting, trash cans —
Trucks, buses, cars, taxicabs —
Traffic flow and signs for control and direction —
Parks, zoos, play areas —
These are all components
of our larger, man-made environment.

Office towers of glass and concrete
that reach dozens of floors into the sky —
Houses, apartments, condominiums, industrial parks —
Municipal buildings, courthouses,
schools, colleges, universities,
hospitals and other public institutions —
Churches, cathedrals, temples and synagogues.
These, too, are elements in our man-made environment.

Smooth pipe and sturdy structure are inviting to young climbers.

A dramatic rendering, felt pen and watercolor by Tibor Karsi, for The Pointe (condominium), Isle of Wight, Ocean City, Maryland; Meyers and D'Aleo, Inc., architects and planners, Baltimore, Maryland.

The roughened surface of the free-form sculpture offers a delightful contrast with the elegant and sophisticated architectural structure of glass and concrete. Banque Lambert Office Building and Residence, Brussels, Belgium; Skidmore, Owings and Merrill, architects. Photograph by Ezra Stoller, courtesy of AIA Information Service, Washington, D.C.

Man is a builder.
He builds small forms, big forms and bigger forms —
Structures that enclose space —
Specific space in which to live
and grow and relax;
Space in which to transact business
and to conduct the process of government —
Space where a seemingly countless variety
of products may be manufactured
to meet the needs of society —
Man constructs places for worship,
for recreation and education
and for the health and welfare of people.

Detail showing texture of masonry wall of split face corduroy block; International Brotherhood of Electrical Workers Local No. 24 building, Meyers and D'Aleo, architects and planners, Baltimore, Maryland.

A series of contrasting textures, open space and flora capture the flavor of a tropical resort hotel. Mauna Kea Beach Hotel, Kamuela, Hawaii; Skidmore, Owings and Merrill, architects. Photograph by R. Wenkam, courtesy of AIA Information Service, Washington, D.C.

61

The Gas Light Tower and the Regency Hyatt House viewed through the sculpture, "The Renaissance of the City," Atlanta, Georgia. Photograph courtesy of Bell and Stanton, Inc., Public Relations.

The attraction of this environmental combination is not only the contrast in forms but the variation in textures.

Man tears down the old, forgotten structures and builds new monuments to the future. This process reveals a wide variety of textures in the rubble of destroyed buildings that contrast with the sense of organization in new architecture.

The cycle of rebuilding goes on. Even the air is textured by dust as the wrecker's ball, swinging in steady pendulum — like fashion, batters an ancient landmark into a mere memory.

Man is a maker of things —
Television sets, dishwashers, toasters,
Chairs, lamps, tables,
Pots and pans —
Draperies, wallpaper, tiles and rugs —
Clothes and countless accessories —
Automobiles, bicycles and a Honda —
Computers and duplicators
and thousands of other things
that have functional or decorative purposes —
or a combination of both.

Each of these man-made components
of our complex world —
big or small,
fifty floor office tower or miniature transistor radio —
has a TEXTURE of its own,
depending upon the materials with which it is made.

Look at the illustrations on these pages —
creations of the architect, the stylist, the designer.
How many different TEXTURES do you see?
How does TEXTURE enhance?
Attract?
Provide specific appeal?

Covered serving dishes, stainless steel; Manufacturer: George Jensen, Ltd., Denmark. Designer, Magnus Stephenson, Danish. Phyllis B. Lambert fund. The Museum of Modern Art, New York.

The contrasting shiny and dull finishes are achieved by the way in which the metal is treated.

Photograph courtesy of Herman Miller, Inc., Zeeland, Michigan. The course woven fabric sets up an interesting contrast with the smooth metal legs.

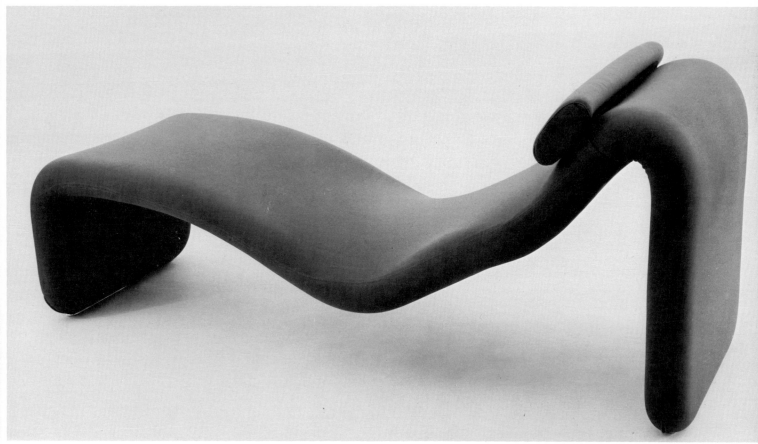

Chaise, nylon stretch fabric over foam rubber on steel frame. Manufacturer: Airborne International, France. Designer, Olivier Mourgue. Gift of George Tanier, Inc., New York. The Museum of Modern Art, New York.

67

The fabric cover gives a soft, velvety feeling to this piece of furniture.

Detail, interior textures of a new car. Photograph courtesy of General Motors Corporation.

*New XEROX 9200 Duplicating System with smooth surfaces and efficient operation
can duplicate and collate original documents at the rate of two impressions a second.*

Interior, Chase Manhattan Bank, New York City. Photograph courtesy of Skidmore, Owings and Merrill, New York. A combination of textures, all pleasing, make this a pleasant place to await an appointment.

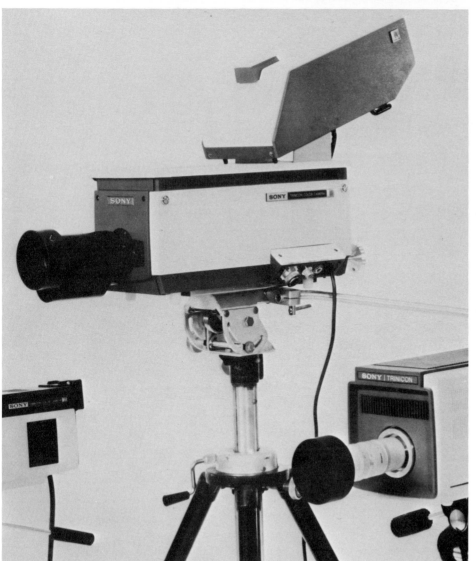

"TRINICON" color Video Camera. Photograph courtesy of Sony Corporation of America. Smooth surfaces mean pleasant handling of this TV equipment.

Wood siding, stucco over concrete block, glass, outdoor furniture, gravel court and planting result in interesting textural contrasts. Deer Point (townhouses), Ocean City, Maryland. Meyers and D'Aleo, Inc., architects and planners, Baltimore, Maryland. Photograph by Otto Baitz.

Atlantis (Condominium), architect's model, Ocean City, Maryland. Meyers and D'Aleo, architects and planners, Baltimore, Maryland. Contemporary, bold and smooth, this building will depend on its completeness by the textural qualities introduced through planting.

This book on TEXTURE ends here. But it also begins at this point as you continue to develop your understanding of TEXTURE, along with the other design elements (line, shape, form, color, value and space), and how it is an integral part of your daily life.

You are looking down a 2200-foot macadam runway, Fallston Airport, Maryland. Important to the safe landing of an airplane, is a smooth, flat airstrip, such as this.

Acknowledgments: My thanks to all those who assisted me by providing photographic material to illustrate this manuscript, including: AIA Information Service, Washington, D.C.; Andre Lemieux, representative for Jordi Bonet, Canadian artist; Bill Meyers of Meyers and D'Aleo, Inc., architects and planners, Baltimore, Maryland; The Baltimore Museum of Art; General Motors Corporation; Herman Miller, Inc.; Bell and Stanton, Inc., Public Relations, Atlanta, Georgia; Museum of Contemporary Crafts, New York; The Museum of Modern Art, New York; Skidmore, Owings and Merrill, Architects, New York; Sony Corporation of America; Xerox Corporation.